The Prodigal Son

Copyright© 2019 Jeffrey Briscoe

All rights reserved. This book or any portion thereof may not be reproduced, distributed, or transmitted in any form or by any means, including photocopying, recording, or other electronic or mechanical methods, without the prior written permission of the publisher, except in the case of brief quotations embodied in critical reviews and certain other non-commercial uses permitted by copyright law. For permission, write to the publisher at the email below.

ISBN: 978-1-951614-00-3 (Paperback)

Library of Congress Control Number: 01-8220932621

Front cover image by Ebony Lynnel Harris

Book design by Ebony Lynnel Harris

Printed by BE Publishing Company in the United States of America.

First print, 2019

BE Publishing, Baltimore MD tgstworkshops@gmail.com

The Prodigal Son

Jeffrey Briscoe Sr.

DEDICATION

This book is dedicated to my late mother Edith M. L. Briscoe and my spiritual mother the late Pastor Violet Shird.

"Have mercy upon me, O God, according to thy lovingkindness: according unto the multitude of thy tender mercies blot out my transgressions." Psalms 51:1

Table Of Contents

Table Of Contents 7

Foreward 9

Preface: The importance of 'The Prodigal Son' and its meaning ... 13

Acknowledgements 19

The darkest day of my life 21

Slow Fade 27

Giving up on Everything 35

How did I get here? 41

The road back home 47

Overcoming self 53

People don't forget 59

When a process meets a promise 65

Unconditional love 71

New life 79

A call to self evaluation 83

A challenge to change 89

Sponsor 98

Foreward

Am I really grateful? This question looms in the minds and hearts of believers of Jesus Christ. This is a humbling experience to submit this forward to this book, for this has everything to do with my relationship to the Almighty Father. I have authored two books and am excited about the content of this book. This story of the Prodigal son takes place in St. Luke 15:11-32, and relates to our lives today. Many have come to God broken, desperate, fearful, and hopeless; yet have looked for Him to establish an equilibrium in their lives that they lacked. As in this story, once God has answered their cry and responded to healing their brokenness and providing for them, many forget the promises that were made previously. When God blesses many with substance, they become reckless with the blessings of God that were not labored for but granted. One might submit that the heart of man can easily use and forget the labor of love extended when someone changes their situation for them. Therein lies the problem. The situation is changed; yet not the person's habits, behavior, or heart. Without this being addressed honestly, we will never be grateful; yet live in the expectancy of someone always being there to bail us out of life experiences. One should never overlook the responsibilities of life to expect others to enable them through situations.

In this story of the Prodigal son, many focus their attention on the ending where the son is restored by his father back into the family. It does not show gratitude on behalf of the son, just relief on behalf of the father. One must be sure to search the content of their heart to find the motives that cause the action to be set in motion. At that time, look for help if need be to confront and conquer the issue so that gratitude can be your outcome. Jeff Briscoe, the author of this book, is full of gratitude after the struggle of life that plagued him. It was more than just being accepted by God that moved his heart, yet it was the gratitude that God would still do away with his past and present him a glorious future. This is so impactful and necessary to every reader God will not only accept you where you are; yet help you confront what you are running from and then put you in a safe place. This is what God has done for me. We all have been in a place where we thought life had won, and many did not want to continue, but God accepted us back in our confused, hurt, broken, and lifeless state. This is where God does his best work. He allows one the grace to gather themselves, the guidance to face themselves, and the love to come and be with Him. What you will see in this book are the real-life hardships that one can live through and the ability to set one's heart and overcome all obstacles. I encourage all that read this to evaluate your life and question yourself, "Am I really grateful?" God bless you in your reading.

Apostle Charles Waters,
3rd Heart of Worship Ministries

Preface: The importance of 'The Prodigal Son' and its meaning

Most people look at books named after stories found in the Bible and keep going. I know I'm guilty of it myself. After all, if you wanted to hear the story, it could be read from the Bible. Right? I thought the same thing until one day I found myself living it. I heard many say, "History repeats it's self." Something else I found to be true. The story of the Prodigal Son is the story of a Father's love for His child (children). Every one of us can put ourselves in this place because all have sinned and fallen short of the glory of God. In my short time on this earth, I learned that knowing the penalty is not enough to keep you from falling into sin. I knew the consequences, but I kept falling over and over again.

There was a time where I walked with God. Some could say that I had things good. The Lord was using me in the ministry to preach, prophesy, and pray for His people. The Bible says that pride goes before destruction, and this was true in my case. I got to a place where I became so confident in myself and comfortable in the abilities that God gave me that I began lacking and didn't even realize it. God was no longer the center of my attention. I put trust in myself and what I could do, failing to realize that I was only a steward of what He gave me. Like the prodigal son, eventually, I lost what was precious to me. I'm not talking about material things, but the presence of God in my life. I know some of you may be thinking, "how can you lose the presence of God?" I know He's everywhere, but I lost it! I'm here to tell someone that backsliding doesn't happen overnight. It's a true saying that the little foxes destroy the vine. When I lost focus, the enemy crept in, and eventually, after choosing my will over His will, I realized I was so deep in sin, and I thought I had no way out, but God. That is why it is vital to submit to God.

James 4:7 says,
"Submit yourselves therefore to God.
Resist the devil, and he will flee from you."

My last sermon was when I was only 28 years old, and I will never forget that day. Afterward, I went to a house where I had a conversation with a young lady and eventually ended up in a hotel room. The vivid picture still plagues my mind reminding me of what happens when you choose your will over His. It was as if a torrential rain had unlocked, which God restrained for moments like this. I saw God sobbing for me as the thunder echoed through the sky, and the storm fell to the earth. Yes, it was raining heavy, causing a sense of urgency for numerous souls as they rushed desperately in search of shelter lest they washed away in that great downpour caused by my rebellion.

Not only was I disappointed in myself, I felt that God shared the same feelings for me. I no longer have to imagine how King Saul felt when the presence of the Lord departed from him. I had to live it with its daily torment. When I would look back at it, I reasoned within myself. I obeyed the rules, made sure I smiled and did my best to be the strong one. I got tired, and like the prodigal son who went to his father demanding his portion ahead of time, I felt entitled to the things restricted from me.

I want someone to realize, I was slowly fading, but the blessing of the Lord was still on my life. The Lord was using me, and souls were being saved and delivered. I went from a state of being blessed to what I could only describe as graceless. I never thought it would lead me away that far, and all so I could enjoy the pleasures of sin for a season. I moved from the original inheritance that God had given me and chose to indulge in things that I would generally avoid. I began to revert to my former ways, going to clubs, hanging out, adultery, things that should not be named once among a child of God, but yet I was still His child, even though I wasn't acting like it.

How should I use this book?

I want people to see the Prodigal. It's more than a story and about more than just the son and his behavior. This book is to encourage someone never to overlook how much love God has for us; He loves us more than we can ever comprehend. I'm not saying that God accepts sin, but His Love covers a multitude of faults. Romans 3:23 lets us know that all fall short of the glory of God. All means everyone, so remember His power can still reach you where you are, even in your low place. The reality is when we measure ourselves to the perfect law of God; we see that we keep falling short over and over again. I feel this book will help someone. Maybe you are hiding, trying to stay as far away from God, and anything that resembles Him. You may be contemplating suicide, whatever your circumstances, come to God just as you are and He can mend your brokenness.

Acknowledgements

I want to give a special thank you to my wife, Sharelle Briscoe, and all of my children for loving me and not leaving me while I was in this experience. Also, to my siblings, your love and support mean a lot to me, you know I don't look like the storm I've been through; To my pastor Bishop Harris for your leadership and guidance at a very delicate time in my life.

The darkest day of my life

I can't tell you the exact time, but I believe it was in the fall of 2006. I was with a few associates in the O'Donnel Heights area, walking back and forth from the Baltimore Travel America truck stop to what used to be my neighborhood. I don't want to sugar coat anything; I went from preaching to men and women, compelling them to turn from sin to selling drugs in a truck stop. I was walking with two other men as a group of men wearing face masks approached us. There wasn't some epic chase that leads to me getting away by the skin of my teeth, although one of the two men who were with me got away. It was two grown men, scared to death surrounded with no logical way out.

Looking back, this had to be the darkest day of my life. It wasn't because they surrounded us. I can remember feeling this intense fear, something that I had masked for so long. And the dread of what was to come felt unbearable, I wished

I could turn back the hands of time. I had no retreat, only this fearful expectation that ironically, I used to preach about to others. My heart was beating inside my chest as if it were about to jump right out. No, this was not the time to have a poker face, not when your standing so close to eternity and unready to enter in.

A man from among them told us, "get down on your knees!" He was the only one without a face mask, holding a gun, demanding that we follow his instructions and turn our backs to him. He planned to kill us execution-style. I was far from God, and in His mercy, He helped me to see that if I got on my knees, I was going to die. So, I did not do it. Looking back, I feared what was to come more than the men standing in front of me.

My friend and I were both trying to talk ourselves out of the situation; it seemed like to no avail. Don't you know God will come to disrupt your plans to bring you back to where you are supposed to be? If you don't believe me, look at Jonah. He thought he was safe on the ship traveling in the opposite direction, and God sent a great fish to put him back on track. It not only frightened Jonah, but it made everyone around him start praying. Like Jonah, I was going in the wrong direction, and you better believe I was praying that day, praying that my life would not expire, not like this. Waisted potential, with all that God put in me, fear mounted up inside me. The man began to reach in my pockets, pulling out fake money, and in the midst of this, I was pleading for my life, telling the man that I was a preacher. I pulled out a picture of my son, who was still an infant and showed it to him, praying to appeal to his humanity for mercy. I was a backsliding preacher about to get killed for selling drugs. I knew I was going to hell if they killed me. I had a God moment in that dark place of my life. Earlier that day, I only wanted to make money. I had an agenda, which was my own, and it did not include God. I thought I was happy living in adultery with a baby out of wedlock, riotous living as the Bible would put it. What happens when you consistently ignore God, who is trying to call you back to Him. Sometimes He gives you another chance, but that's not guaranteed. A dangerous game of Russian-roulette.

We walked back and forth a few times that day and wasn't aware that our every move was being watched. These were just men, but God never took His eyes off of us. Sin had its pleasures, and before that moment, I was enjoying them, but as the Bible says in James 1:15, when sin is finished, it brings forth death. Living in a backslidden condition, I relished the pleasures, but there was this indescribable pain caused by the separation, that robbed me of peace. At that moment, my hope leaving, it all boiled down to one man. Was he going to display kindness and mercy and let us go or if he was going to show others not to trespass? Although I thought this was my end, and that God had given up on me, God had mercy on me, and the men let us go. I say God because I know that the heart of the King is in God's hand. I know someone was praying for me. That's why it's important to pray for those who are backsliders when God puts someone on your heart to pray for them, don't hesitate, they might be at the point of death. I appreciate all those who prayed for my safe return to the Kingdom; your labor of love is not in vain. It sounds cliche, but as long as you have breath in your body, it may not be too late. Don't let the fear of your past stop you from coming back to your Father. People can't place you in heaven or hell; that's not their place. I would later realize that God was trying to call me back home, back in a right relationship with Him.

After a few days, as the evil spirit came over Saul's mind, overwhelming his judgment until his body somehow responded, with hate, pride seemed to consume me when I should have felt gratefulness. The funny thing about doing a criminal act and not wearing a mask, you can be recognized later. I'm not glorifying the enemy, but I am exposing him for what he tried to do to me even after God delivered me with a mighty hand.

It was only days later that I saw that same unmasked man walk to the school right across the street from my house to pick up a child. Yes, the enemy was talking to my mind, I wanted revenge, but at the same time, this was also a test. Would I show mercy to the same person who gave me mercy? Although I was upset, I never did anything, and he wasn't even aware that I was watching him. Don't get me wrong, the desire for revenge and to retaliate was strong; after all, this was my pride that was hurting. It had to be God's mercy looking out for me when my judgment was clouded because pride is a dangerous thing. I think of the parable of the unforgiving servant Jesus describes in Matthew 18:21-35. If it wasn't for the mercy of God, that could have been me.

It didn't happen overnight, but after a while, I began to cry out to God for help. All I wanted was to be out of sin and have the relationship that I used to have with Him. I missed that, I desperately wanted to be out of sin, but I didn't go back to church. I was secretly wounded, and it would be many more years before I got my life back together. Some of the deepest wounds are the ones that cannot be seen, which ironically take the longest to heal. I was away from God so long I started to believe everything that the enemy was telling me. Hurt, desperately desiring God, yet it seemed as if others only watched from the poolside as I was in the process of drowning. I know I went against the rules and jumped in, but I was in desperate need of mercy. I received a great deliverance, my life spared, yet I still felt worthless. That's just like the devil to make you think God doesn't want you after He proves His love to you over and over again.

Slow Fade

Saints of God, did you know you could backslide in your heart before doing it outwardly? Yes, It came to my mind before I did it. I was so confident in myself that I thought I had it all. I believe that's when my heart began to fade away from God slowly. I thought I was spiritual, but the truth is I was carnal.

Proverbs 23:7 says,
"For as he thinketh in his heart, so is he: Eat and drink, saith he to thee; but his heart is not with thee."

II started working as a valet manager, and I began to slack in fasting, praying, and feeding my natural man instead of the spiritual man. I engaged with the employees acting more like them, and I got sidetracked. When you get distracted, you forget what real joy and happiness is. It's like looking at yourself in a mirror when you turn away; you forget how you look. I turned away from God, and I forgot that His wages were fair. I started to desire a different type of joy and happiness. We have to be careful because the devil is cunning. God told Adam and Eve that they would surely die; the enemy came behind and said something different. There is a revelation in that scripture. When God tells you something, it is good to take heed, the enemy knows his time is short, and he is out to get as many of us off track as he can. God sees beyond what we do.

One of the female employees started showing me affection, and my flesh desired to be satisfied. It's nothing new; this flesh always wants to be pleased, and we know that no good thing dwells in this flesh. I used to hear some of the seasoned saints of God saying, "If you don't fast, you won't last," and "if you don't pray, you won't stay." This saying is right every time; everyone who desires to live holy must remember that we will never make it to a point where the basics don't apply to us, no matter how good you are at what you do.

We are instructed to guard our hearts with all diligence, laying hold to anything contrary to the will of God. In doing so, we cast down everything that tries to exalt itself in our lives against God. Someone needs to know that this didn't happen all at once. It progressed over time. The enemy was slowly leading me further away; I had no idea that I would end up losing so much; I didn't see it coming. You can't play with the enemy, and if you give him an inch, he will take a mile. We know his plan, God told us that he was coming to steal, kill, and destroy, believe it. My advice to all who would listen, I encourage people to pray; Jesus Himself quoted that, "men ought always to pray, and not to faint;" Even if you feel like you don't want to go to church, keep your communication with God open. Don't let people stop you from going to your Father's house. God is our Father (Our), and nothing should be able to separate us from the love of God. He is our Father; even earthly fathers talk to their children when they are upset with them, is God not greater?

2 Chronicles 7:14 says,
"If my people, which are called by my name, shall humble themselves, and pray, and seek my face, and turn from their wicked ways; then will I hear from heaven, and will forgive their sin, and will heal their land."

Don't feel like God won't hear you. No matter what you are struggling with, there is a war going on, and if you can humble your self and pray and seek God's face, then God will hear you. Just don't try to be proud. Remember who you are and who He is. Let me tell you, God, the creator of the ends of the earth, knows everything, the ending from the beginning.

Don't you think He knew you were going to mess up, He knew, and He prayed for you that your faith fails not. My story is a perfect example of what happens to a man who falls into sin, and their faith fails, but God.

Many have heard the story of Jonah, who was a distinguished preacher. Well, this preacher ran from God, he didn't want to do the will of God because he was prejudice and questioned God's mercy, yet he is still considered great. We learn that Jesus is the expressed image of God, and we cannot question His ways. Nor can we tell men and women that God is different. When I look at Jesus in the Bible, I see a God of mercy and love and forgiveness. God is not waiting to judge you; He desires to love you and bring you to an expected end.

Jeremiah 29:11 says,
"For I know the thoughts that I think toward you, saith the LORD, thoughts of peace, and not of evil, to give you an expected end."

While I was in adultery, I wanted out of it. I started to quote this scripture to myself from Psalms 118:17; "I shall not die but live to declare the works of the Lord." I never forgot. God delivered me, and although it was years later, He blessed me to go back to Him, and now I am declaring the word of the Lord again.

God does not want to send the backslider to hell, it's not his will that any of us should perish, but all come to repentance. We get it wrong when we cast judgment on those who have fallen short. God said He is married to the backslider. I know situations make some people feel like they want a divorce, but they don't know what's right for them. Being connected to the world will never be better than being yoked up with God. The devil is a hard taskmaster, he is abusive, and he is secretly jealous of you and desires to kill you.

Marriage takes work, and a good one does not happen overnight. Sometimes you feel like you want to leave. Some couples have been married for what seems to be a lifetime, and they genuinely enjoy each other. It is because they decided to stay together through the thick and the thin, choosing to work things out even when it didn't look like what they wanted. The ones who are willing to stay focused, those are the ones that stay together.

James 1:13-15 says,

"Let no man say when he is tempted, I am tempted of God: for God cannot be tempted with evil, neither tempteth he any man: But every man is tempted, when he is drawn away of his own lust, and enticed. Then when lust hath conceived, it bringeth forth sin: and sin, when it is finished, bringeth forth death."

When looking at our circumstances, we get an Elijah complex and immediately start to feel like we are in this thing all by ourselves. As if our sin caught the God who knows the end from the beginning by surprise. You are not the only one that God ever saved, and you are not the only backslider in this world. At one point, all of Israel was a backslider, yet God redeemed them over and over again. The opposition will continue to come until the day you leave this earth; you have to have an all or nothing attitude. If I were you, I would pray that God allows me to have a bounce-back spirit. Lord, whatever happens, help me to get back up and do it again, help me to focus on you and not my situation. Jesus is the perfect example that we should pray before it happens.

Luke 22:32 says,

But I have prayed for thee, that thy faith fail not: and when thou art converted, strengthen thy brethren.

Jesus prayed for us not that we don't fail, but that our faith does not fail while failing and making our way back to Him. How can I say that? Jesus was talking to Peter, a man who He knew was about to deny Him three times, run, hide, and return to the life that he was told to leave. Jesus knew that Judas would betray Him, and all of the disciples would forsake Him, yet He invested in them and entrusted the disciples to look after His sheep. God wasn't looking at what they were, but what they could be because He saw their potential as a reality.

He told the parables of the lost sheep, who wanders off, and the shepherd leaves the 99 sheep that are safe to seek the one who was lost. Then there is the parable of the woman who lost a coin of great value. Don't you know you are valuable to God! And last is the story that this book is about, the lost son. When a soul that has lost their way has found their way back to the Father, there is great joy in heaven.

Luke 15:7 says,
I say unto you, that likewise joy shall be in heaven over one sinner that repenteth, more than over ninety and nine just persons, which need no repentance.

God will not tempt you, nor will He make you live right. He will, however, allow you to make your own decisions and help you get it right when you decide to yield to Him. Saints watch! If you find yourself having little interest in going to the house of God, praying, fasting, or reading the Word of God, this may be your slow fade. If you find yourself in that state, you are in desperate need of a spiritual revival. If I were you, I would start crying out to God like never before; some people who go out, don't make it back into the ark of safety.

Giving up on Everything

Have you ever been at a point where you felt so low, you felt like you couldn't get back up? In my backsliding state, I felt ashamed, worthless, like I wanted to die and go to hell and get it over. I was in a great depression, a low point in my life. My struggle was that I could not pray for myself and that God was not going to hear me. I thought I could not go to God and say anything, I knew He was holy and righteous, and I felt dejected, how could I approach God.

I had this desire to talk to God, but I felt that He wasn't going to hear me until He opened my understanding to see that He always hears me. As long as I repent, God will listen to and answer my prayer.

In this experience, I learned that God was able to keep me not only on the mountain, but He also kept me in the valley too. Even in a mess that I got myself into, God was still preserving me for this time. Yes, God will also keep you while you are going through your mess. God was still dealing with me while I was in my backslidden condition. Don't think that God won't deal with a backslider, because they are doing the wrong thing; we don't serve a God like that. I gave up on everything, and then I got tired of giving up over and over again, so I decided to leave. Walking away from God is always a personal decision.

We have to be willing to change so that His ways become our ways. We can't be so caught up with a protocol that we fail to see the souls crying out to God. It may be offering time, but if God has revealed to you that a sheep needs His help, we have to get rid of our program and go to the sheep. Jesus came to seek and to save those who were lost, and we can't be so caught up with a custom that we let sheep continue to fall prey to the wolves and fall into ditches. The only way people can have restoration is that we step out of our traditions and how we think it should go.

No one should leave church feeling hopeless, not when they come to the place of deliverance. On the one hand, we preach love and repentance, but yet we can't get past the sin they did years ago. Then if we do forgive them, we set timelines for their liberation like wait five years or three years to preach again or to be on the choir because you sinned. God forgives us a lot faster than His people do. That's why His thoughts are not like ours. Forgiveness goes deeper than just saying I forgive you. Some people will hate you because you sinned against God, you did nothing to them, but they can't forgive you. It's time to get things right in the body of God.

Don't be guilty of causing people to feel unworthy and go back on God all over again. In my case, I felt judged. Can you imagine getting your nerve together to come back to the house of God to be told that God forgives me and that I can work towards restoration? Only to not be used by God and have to sit down as if I'm this broke down monument only observed for the wrong I've done. Yes, I fell, but I needed restoration in the spirit of Love.

We need to be careful about how we are dealing with forgiveness. I can understand if a person chooses to live in sin and they don't want to give it up, that person needs to be set down. A person who has repented and seeks deliverance need not wait long periods before they work in God's house. An idle mind is the devil's workshop. It's not good for anyone to sit in God's house idle, they may have to usher, or do something, but it gives your mind time to wonder, and that is not what you need when you are trying to stay focused. People of God, we have to do better. God is calling us higher. I was sinking deep in sin, and many only watched from a distance the tragedy, God is looking for someone who will stand in the gap and show love, after all, isn't that how others know who we are, by the love we have one for another.

Repentance is not a twelve-step program; it is only one step. The lowest place in my life was the most beautiful experience for me. Sure, I didn't see it, but looking back, it was in my weakness that I learn who God was and who I was in Him. I heard it said, when you hit rock bottom, the only place to go is up. I didn't just hit rock bottom, I laid there and wallowed in self-pity and guilt until God showed me that He still had a plan for my life, which included my brokenness. Yes, it was a beautiful place, if I never hit bottom, I would not have known the depth of His love for me, nor could I understand the reach of His compassion that He has for the backslider. I can relate to the person who walked away from God; maybe they feel all is lost as if they can never be saved. I can tell that person that there is hope.

In Luke, the 7th chapter, Mary, a sinner, comes to Jesus and anoints His feet with precious oil and washes His feet with her hair. As the Pharisees who were with him began to complain, Jesus tells a story of two debtors. One of them owed five hundred denarii, and the other only owed fifty. The master forgave both servant's debt. Jesus then asked, "Who do you think will love the master more?" His question was answered, "The one whom he forgave the most." God not only forgives us our trespasses, but he cast it into the sea of forgiveness.

Saints of God lets not be insensitive to the souls that are crying out for deliverance; maybe you can't see how a person can walk away from God, or how they can fall so far into sin. Remember, if not for His mercy, that could have been you. Sure, you may say you would never walk away from God now, but trust what I say, every word you say will be tested, so make sure you can back up what you say. We emphasize the backsliders who walk away from the church building, but what of the ones that backslide and never leave the four walls. Maybe you have backslidden on the low, and you want to keep your sin hush, lest the condemnation of man consume you. Just in case you were wondering, yes, you are a prodigal, as well.

All have sinned and fallen short of the glory of God; it is in man's nature to sin. The question is, are we able to love as Jesus loves us? At what point do we stop pretending that we never sinned and let people know that even if they fall, we are proof that you can get back up again. Just in case I lost someone, all unrighteousness is a sin.

How did I get here?

As I stated previously, the transition from my mountain to my valley didn't happen overnight. It was a slow fade. I was in the church building, but I was at a spiritual standstill. I was no longer progressing but regressing in the spirit, which eventually manifested in my daily walk, leading me to walk away from God. My backsliding began the moment I stopped growing in God, but it would be many years before I realized this truth.

When I first walked away from God, I started running women. This flesh will have you all messed up; there is no good thing that dwells in anyone's flesh. I was still working, and I had this one friend that was a drug dealer. I stopped desiring the things of God and started preoccupying my mind with what I could gain to please my flesh. You are always moving, either its towards God or away from Him. No exceptions, you are never at a standstill. I desired that fast life with money and women, the one that the enemy glorifies through society. I asked this individual over and over for drugs to sell, but he didn't want to give me anything. My friend told me that he was ducking me out, and he didn't want to get in trouble with God by putting drugs in my hand. I now realize how much of a good friend he was. He was concerned about my wellbeing, wanting me to come out of my calamity.

It seems like I should have gotten the picture; God was trying to help me and send me back in the right direction. The thing is when someone has a mindset that is against God; it's hard to change them. That's why King David had to ask God, create in me a clean heart. The cares of this world can turn you entirely against God. After a while, I got in touch with another friend who was hesitant at first then he started giving me drugs to sell. I started selling marijuana, and I even had people selling drugs under me, that entrepreneurial spirit that God placed in me was now being used to build up the kingdom of the enemy.

I'm going to tell you how bad the devil had my mind. I had come to a point where I fell into despair, I didn't see hope for myself, and when you don't see hope for yourself that's when the enemy gets happy, he got you right where he wants you. How are you going to see that there is hope for others if you don't have that hope for yourself? I'm telling this story not to glorify the enemy; someone needs to see how far the enemy will lead you away if you get distracted. If you feel like you can come to why you think is a standstill, while all along you are slipping away from the destiny that God has for you. One day while I was in the middle of my mess, I had one guy who called me crying. He said he wanted to be a Christian like me; he was coming to me so I could lead him to God. The problem was, I needed someone to lead me to God as well. I was walking around feeling hopeless in my spirit, and instead of me connecting him with someone who could help him, I became selfish and asked him if I could buy drugs from him. Misery loves company. Yes, the devil had me right where he wanted me, and I was working for him. We might think that we will never do certain things; we don't know what the enemy is going to have us to do when we walk away from God. He wants to parade fallen soldiers because if we can't make it, how can anyone else.

See the enemy his desire is for you and every soul God has assigned to come to Him through you to die in sin. That young man that I asked to buy drugs from, eventually ended up dying. He was found dead in someone elses basement. The same man who cried out, saying he wanted to give his life to God. Looking back, I had become an enemy of the cross of Christ. My God had become my appetite to satisfy my flesh. The memory of this situation is something that I live with to this day, the cost of my disobedience. Souls are too importance; your soul is everything you have, its the only thing you have control over. Every life is valuable in God's eyes, and it should be in ours too. People are counting on you to do the right thing, and their lives depend on it.

I can't begin to tell you the guilt I felt, I could have helped him, yet he stayed in his situation because I decided that I wanted to live carnally one day. Sure it started small, but in the end, it cost a life, and although I knew it was my fault, it would be years before I came back to God. Walking around with guilt and shame is not an easy thing, but even they have a purpose. Guilt is the heaviness that you feel in your conscience when you have done wrong. It is meant to lead us to a place of repentance so our sins can be blotted out, not to have us walking around defeated with our heads hung down. Yes, it hurts, but we have to be able to get back up again. Shame is the feeling of hurt because you failed to live up to an ideal standard. They work together, and when you feel guilty, it leads you to repent. Then when you remember the shame, you are less likely to return to do that thing again. So both guilt and shame have a purpose, not that we are consumed by it, unable to function correctly, but that we use it to learn and grow, that we don't repeat the same mistakes.

Sin has a way of keeping you locked in, it feels good, and its only when you have your mind made up to do the right thing, that you stand a fighting chance. It's hard to fight if you don't want to. I want to plead with someone today. Your friends and family depend on you to stay saved. They might not say it, but it would break some of them if you fell. I continued to live for the devil, and I was on a chat line one night, which lead to me meeting my son Jacobs mother. She lived in the O'Donnel Heights area, where I had the moment that changed everything.

The road back home

I have to repeat it, people of God, we over complicate things. Repentance is and has only ever been one step. It requires you to turn around, all the way around — a 180-degree turn. I desired to be free, I began to love God all over again, and I wanted to come back home. I started going from church to church, talking to different pastors. Not that I was church hopping, but looking for acceptance and deliverance. I had a confession that I wanted to give, and during my journey, I developed a relationship with God all over again. Already I had begun a turnaround in my mind; I began to desire the things of God more than I wanted the elements of the world. My sorrow for my trespasses, lead to repentance. I want to help someone; repentance is a gift; it should never be forced, it is a willing sacrifice, not of money but a broken spirit; a broken and contrite heart. When you come to the Father with the right kind of mindset, He will receive you with open arms.

During the time that I was visiting churches, a pastor told me that God would give me a church home. I didn't just want to visit a church every Sunday; I was looking for a place, one where I belonged. I went to Restoration Ministries, and God not only restored me, But He also called me to this ministry. God used the presiding pastor to tell me to forgive myself, something I had yet to do. I found myself seeking forgiveness from many pastors and churches, but it wasn't until I had forgiven myself that change happened; that is when I felt God reaching back to me, and the shadow of guilt and shame that hovered over me dissipated. Doors began to open, God restored everything that I lost, and blessings overtook me. It was as if God was confirming and reconfirming that He still loved me, and He was with me. The fast money that I was looking for was nothing compared to the overflow that God had for me. He started giving me supernatural blessings.

God has given me a mind to keep moving. I know now that when you go back to the Father's house, He will be waiting for you. Looking back on my exit out of my wilderness experience, I see that relationship made the difference. Having a connection with God, not the one you display on Sunday morning when God's people are watching you; this one is outside the church, it happens when no one else is around. It's never been about a building; you have to be a member of the body of Christ. It has nothing to do with a church building; you are born into this church. How do you get a relationship with God? It starts with a conversation, spending time, dedication, it does not happen overnight, but when you are faithful in your communication, one day, you will see the relationship bloom, and God will be more than an acquaintance, but a Friend.

We live in a generation where everyone wants things instant. People try to rush the process with everything, but God has a set time and a purpose for all things under heaven. I'm not saying I had to fall into sin, I made my choices, and God, who saw the options I picked, decided that He would redeem me. I know I sinned, but He wasn't through with me. I believe I had to learn God, I went through the muck and the mire, and when God brought me out, I now know His mercy and love. I appreciate Him more than I did before. I only shared a little of my story, in my case, God forgave much, so in my gratitude, I love Him deeper. The road back home was not easy, but Jesus Christ, the righteous judge, He was advocating for me, and He prayed for me before this happened, that my faith fails not. I had to deal with reproof, for whom the Lord loves, He corrects. I realized that God was dealing with me as a son, one of His dear children, bringing restoration to my soul.

It's essential not only to be in church but to get your confession out. Confession is good for the soul. I learned that many get stuck on confessing only; it means nothing without forsaking your sin and forgiving yourself. If you don't plan on abandoning your sins, why should you confess them? Yes, the first step to overcoming is acknowledging you have a problem, but there are practicing alcoholics that recognize they have a problem. We have to give God something to work with and keep going until our healing. Maybe you desire to do right, but it's hard for you. Your prayer should be, Lord, create in me a clean heart. Everyone goes through a process, love yourself during your journey to wholeness and seek God for strength to walk away from anything that is not like Him. Repentance and restoration should happen daily; we are always going to God to make sure we are in right standing with Him.

In the Bible, we see that the father (who represents God) wasn't worried about the son's past but that he was coming home. Many don't believe that God can restore and save them, so the enemy tricks the minds of people to think that things are over. The adversary was talking to me, telling me that I was too old and that I waisted too much time in the world. The enemy may be trying to use your past against you, but the Bible instructs us to be sober or clear-headed. I know people may be talking about you, and you might feel like you don't measure up in the eyes of man, but you are not here for their glory. You may have heard things like, "You are just reaping what you have sown!" and think that God won't help you. If the sun shines on the just and the unjust, why would God forget you. The Bible says the goodness of the Lord should lead to repentance, so if a person sees God's goodness and repents, why should he stop being good? Some of the things that we have heard throughout the years are a little backward, we have to study to show ourselves approved unto God, a workman that needeth not be ashamed, rightly dividing the words of truth.

Whatever God promises you, it doesn't matter how long it takes; it will come to past. Abraham was said to be a man of faith because he trusted God. Do you believe that He is a God that restores, heals, delivers, and redeems His people? The adversary would have you to think that you have to please people to be saved, but they can't keep you. Only God can do that! Like the man that was sitting at the pool in Bethesda, my vision became distorted. I once saw men as trees, now I can see clearly. I want someone to realize what happened here; this wasn't one of the apostles that made clay and put it on the man's eyes; this was Jesus Himself. The man already had a touched from the Lord, but he had to get touched all over again. That lets me know sometimes you might be going through in your mind, or your body to the point where one touch is not enough. Sometimes all we need is another touch from God. I was fighting through depression, unforgiveness, and doubt, but God! He made a way when I felt all hope was gone. He can do that for you too! Is there anything too hard for God?

Overcoming self

Someone said, "You have to go through until you get to!" This saying is more than a phrase you hear people repeat, it refers to a process, and it takes dedication and trust. God is trying to get us to a place where we learn to put all our faith in Him. It may not happen right away for you, be willing to throw your hands up and say, "Lord, I believe, but help my unbelief." Your reality might show one thing, but God is calling you to believe against reality.

The way we perceive a situation can affect the outcome. When we look at God only as a wrathful God, all-knowing, all-powerful, everywhere at the same time, visiting the iniquity of the fathers upon the sons. We see a vengeful God, how can we expect to receive forgiveness for our trespasses? On the other hand, if we only see God as being good, loving, and kind, forgiving us before anything happens, we might take that as an opportunity to go against His will thinking, I'll be ok, God always forgives. The fact is God is all-powerful and all-knowing, and everywhere at the same time, also loving and kind, and has already provided a way for us at Calvary, not willing that any should perish, but that all come to repentance. He shows us goodness that we might want to repent, and we, in turn, see that we can receive forgiveness. You may not be where you should be; have faith in what God is saying about you. His thoughts are not our thoughts, and His ways are not our ways. When you are battling in your mind, you need to get a proper perspective. What exactly does God say about you?

God says I am made in His image.

Genesis 1:27 says, So God created man in his own image, in the image of God created he him; male and female created he them.

God says that he loves me, not just sometimes, but with an everlasting love.

Jeremiah 31:3 says, The Lord hath appeared of old unto me, saying, Yea, I have loved thee with an everlasting love: therefore with lovingkindness have I drawn thee.

Not only did God make me with a purpose, everything that I go through has a purpose.

Jeremiah 29:11 says, For I know the thoughts that I think toward you, saith the LORD, thoughts of peace, and not of evil, to give you an expected end.

God says I am not just an overcomer; I am more than a conqueror through Him.

Romans 8:37 says, Nay, in all these things we are more than conquerors through him that loved us.

If God says, "You are an overcomer," then you have to take Him at His Word. Stop trying to rush the process, and don't let anyone push you faster than you are supposed to be going. Sometimes God takes you on a journey so you can see more of Him, and in going on that journey, we learn of Him. Favor may show up before money, that's more valuable.

When you have God's favor on your life, you will experience for yourself, that the name of the Lord is a strong tower, and the righteous have a place of refuge in Him. Don't fall victim to the enemy's devices; we have so much going on and get caught up in so much that we forget, Satan is still going around like a roaring lion, even though you came back to God. Your repentance didn't faze him. He is always trying to get you one way or the other. The Bible says, "Who shall separate you from the Love of God?" Are we going to let a preacher or a church member separate us? If you have a relationship, then you should have communication. Talk to God, understand that His thoughts are so much higher than ours will ever be. Everything has a process, even sin. So it's natural that God, our creator, can help us through any process; He did give us an instruction manual, that might be an excellent place to start.

Jeremiah was told to go to the potter's house, and he observed a vessel made of clay, marred in the making. The potter didn't throw it away; he decided to work on it again. Let God be God and let Him work on you all over again! I know it's uncomfortable and you want to get off the wheel, no one likes when they are being tested and tried, but it is a blessing in staying still. The woman caught in adultery; her accusers came to Jesus sinning. Everyone comes to Jesus in sin; He is the only perfect man. Brothers and Sisters in the Lord, let's not cast stones. Let's use this time to work out our salvation with fear and trembling. The late Dr. Martin Luther King Jr. said, If you can't fly, run; If you can't run, walk; If you can't walk, crawl; Whatever you do, don't stop moving.

I know as Saints, some of the difficulties we go through are undesirable; after all, we are only human. Although it's unwanted, remember there is a purpose in you going through your trials and tribulation. There is a process in what you are going through. There is also a promise that you have to obtain.

2 Timothy 3:13 says,
"Yea and all that will live godly in Christ Jesus shall suffer persecution."

Holiness is a suffering way. We should not get upset with Christians when they fall. Our job is to love them and restore them in the spirit of humility. It's too many people dying and going to hell to not show love. I wouldn't want to be the instrument that is used to inflict a fellow brother or sister in the Lord. Saints, we have to be careful of what comes out of our mouth, our actions, Watch, considering how you want to be treated if it were you!

People don't forget

During my short existence on this earth, I have observed a lot. One thing in particular that I feel is detrimental to the Christian walk is our ability to remember. I am not saying that we have a total loss of memory, just selective. No one is exempt from this temptation, even me.

Philippians 3:13-14 says,
Brethren, I count not myself to have apprehended: but this one thing I do, forgetting those things which are behind, and reaching forth unto those things which are before, I press toward the mark for the prize of the high calling of God in Christ Jesus.

Yes, you came to God running for your life, but sometimes you fell and were barely making it, we don't always live on the mountain top. It's so easy for Christians to forget the state they were in before their deliverance. I know we should stay away from sinful things that would cause us to fall into sin. On the other hand, we need never forget how we were once in the same boat as the sinner or the backslider, let's be real with ourselves. In many cases, it could have been us, and in some cases, it was us, everyone hasn't told their stories of deliverance. God has charged me with the awesome responsibility to share what could happen should we choose to be overtaken by pride, I say choose because it is a choice. God is still a keeper. He always has been, you have to want it.

Trying to find my way back into fellowship with the people of God, I ran into many who knew me and didn't forget what I did, even though God forgave me. Yes, it was hurtful, and I wondered why I got the cold shoulder from some. I had to realize; everyone won't love, as God said. See, God is love, and He told us to love one another as He has loved us. God does not play when it comes to Agape Love, and we need it to make it to heaven. I speak to the saint who never walked out on God, don't forget that could have been you if not for the mercy of God. Don't you want to be a vessel of honor, one that edifies, uplifts, and leads by example? Don't you want God to look at these interactions and say, "Well done!"

We have to learn to love ourselves. I'm not talking about showering ourselves with gifts and dressing up, we can do that, but it is more in-depth. I speak to the one who is making their way back to God, do you love yourself enough to forgive those who treat you wrong? The enemy has a job, and it is to get you to turn your back on God. If he can get you to walk out the doors of the church and talk about the people of God for their falling short, you will do just what he wants you to do.

Job 14:7-9 says,

For there is hope of a tree, if it be cut down, that it will sprout again, and that the tender branch thereof will not cease. Though the root thereof wax old in the earth, and the stock thereof die in the ground; Yet through the scent of water it will bud, and bring forth boughs like a plant.

Somewhere, as I am writing this book, as you are reading the words right now, a child of God has fallen, they gave up and are no longer walking according to the will of God. I am not giving a prophecy; this is real life, and it happens every day. Just because people fall doesn't mean that they can't get back up again. It could have been a great fall, isn't the God we serve big enough to pick them up again? If a tree can be cut down and still flourish, not through watering, but the scent of water, how much more for a child of God. God does not throw us away just because we fell short. Even in being the prodigal son, there is hope. I had to learn that sin was what I did, not who I was. When God saved me, I became a son, and being a backslider did not change the fact that I was still a son. I just needed to repent, which should be a daily thing. Everyone, no matter how old you are or how long you have been serving God, has to reconnect with God every day. Don't let what you think people think about you make you feel unworthy.

In some cases, it is accurate, and they do feel that way about you. Then there are some cases it's the enemy trying to attack your mind. His mission is to make you feel like you have no way out. Jesus has always been the only way for every sinner. That includes the homosexual, the whore, the liar, the thief, the backslider, the hypocrite.

Lamentations 3:21-23 says,
This I recall to my mind, therefore have I hope. It is of the Lord's mercies that we are not consumed because his compassions fail not. They are new every morning: great is thy faithfulness.

I'm trying to help someone out of a dark place right now. My brother, my sister, you don't just end up in Hell. You go there because you forget God. The prodigal son didn't forget his father even in his sin; while he was going through, he remembered, he longed to be back at his fathers' house. Not as a son, he would settle for being a servant. Maybe you know a backslider, as long as they don't forget, there is hope. I'm not saying that they can stay in sin and remember God from time to time and make it into heaven in their sin. What I'm saying is when you are mindful of God, sooner or later, you are going to get tired of what the enemy is putting you through, and you're going to start making your way back home.

God still talks to his children, even in their sin. He sends his rain on the just and the unjust. It's hard to forget God in your sin; there is this constant reminder of Him. Don't think every backslider is just having fun and care nothing about God; many are afraid of coming back and dealing with their spiritual siblings. The fear of rejection keeps some of them out because they witnessed it through the years, they saw what happened to various ones who left and attempted to return now they are afraid of what could happen to them. Saint's of God, let's not just do right, let's be right.

When a process meets a promise

Earlier in my life, I had promises spoken to me, and one thing I learned is that God always keeps His promises. I heard the word of the Lord concerning me, but there was a process I had to go through. When you encounter a promise that is declared, you have to go through your process. The process is not to break you, but to break some of the habits you have so that you can be fit for God's use.

When we consider Joseph, I'm sure when he went out to look for his brothers, he had no idea, the day would end with him being led away as a slave to Egypt. Joseph was 17 years old when he received his promise and 37 when it came to pass. Of that time, he spent thirteen years in prison for a crime he had not committed. Twenty years is a long time to wait for a promise. Going from living like a prince, his family was wealthy to being a slave is a significant step backward as it would seem, but He was right where God wanted him to be.

Having to leave the comfort of his home, and serve others, instead of being served, I'm sure he had his moments where he felt, surely the Lord has departed, but he held on to his integrity. When Christ came into my life at 18, before God filled me, He started drawing me closer to Himself.

John 6:44 says,
No man can come to me, except the Father which hath sent me draw him: and I will raise him at the last day.

I went through the new birth experience and a transformation. I learned something; It's easy to say, "you can make it," especially when you are talking from a place of comfort. When you are living in the situation, not being able to see that the battle is won, victory may be the last thing on your mind. It is crucial to trust in God and not in man. We can look at someone's life and think it's messy, but that might be their process. God didn't call us to say how messed up a person is but to love them in the way He intended. It's like we get saved and forget that we were rough around the edges once. God can turn a lump of coal into a diamond, so why not us. It was a time when I felt like I wasn't going to love and smile again; I felt like I was unlovable, hopeless. No matter what anyone says about you, God has the last say, even if it looks impossible, your processes are not always what it seems.

Let's look at the Bible. Starting with the patriarchs, none of them were perfect. Every judge had their baggage, even prophets had their time when they questioned God, every king fell short, even those kings who were considered righteous, and the apostles were only men in need of a savior. We have a habit of placing people on these pedestals; then, when they fall or disappoint us, we feel like, if they can't make it, then I can't either. I am trying to plead with someone today; as long as you have breath in your body, you have hope. There was two other on the cross with Jesus. All three of them were going to die that day. One man reached out to Jesus and said, remember me. Because he trusted, God said, This day thou shall be with me in Paradise. It looked like a hopeless situation. The difference is that one believed that Jesus could help. Whether you believe it or not, you have had a death sentence pronounced over your life. For it is appointed unto man once to die and after that is the judgment. I urge you to cry out to God for mercy; He desires to save you, do you believe He can help you?

Even if your situation is dead, remember the vision that Ezekiel had. It was dry bones. God wanted to show the prophet that though the army had died a long time ago, and their bones were stripped and scattered on the ground, He was not concerned at the way things looked. Yes, the army had been dead for a long time, and there was no reasonable hope for revival. Who can revive a dry bone, but God! He has the ultimate control over every situation. Some things are not dead but delayed. Your life may be at a standstill if you can learn to trust God, you will be alright. He is leading us beside the still waters. Sheep are good swimmers if they don't have a load of heavy wool on them. Being weighed down makes it hard for them to swim, and if they are carrying such a burden, they get alarmed near raging waters. The Lord is our shepherd, and He knows how much we can take at any given time. So when we are going through our toughest times, He will lead us beside still waters. God is concerned with you and me; He desires that we stand still and be sensitive to His will for our life.

Trouble will drive us to God; it's the way life is set up. When you are dealing with God, it is about your communication with Him. God did not intend for us to be on our own, yet it is more critical that we have a relationship with Him than man. Don't neglect God in prayer; we flood to social media the first thing in the morning, yet we forget to say thank you because we opened our eyes. God doesn't need us; we need Him, which should be more of an incentive to say thank you for being able to open your eyes. In Hebrews 11:1, we read that faith is the substance of things hoped for and the evidence of things not seen. If a man is working in a factory, there is a specific order that things go in. The box doesn't fill its self, and there are people in place to make sure the package is complete. One may water, but God gives the increase. Our processes may include some experiencing raped, abuse, a family member or friend dying. These things happen, but it is a process, not the end of the story. The prodigal son is the story of love and forgiveness. This young man went through a process. He realized that it was better to be a servant for his father than to stay in the pigpen. You may be going through your process on today, don't lose focus, because the fulfillment of your promise may be closer than you think.

Unconditional love

We were called to love one another and to be around sinners. I'm not saying that you have to partake in sin, but don't exile the sinner because they are not like you. The people coming into the church aren't the only ones who need to hear the word. What about those on the outside who have yet to listen to the gospel? We are called to go out into the market places, on your jobs, in your communities, in the schools, and on the streets. It's not behind the walls of the church; this is only a training ground; we have to get out. If we seek to only stay in the church, how will the world see our light? Jesus was commonly seen around sinners, not because He wanted to be like them. His presence helped them know what they were missing. If only we could get back to trying to imitate His reflection, then maybe we would stop worrying about the wrong things.

We can't forget the great love that God has for us. God wants to reconcile the world back to Himself, and it's through the church. But we have to go back and do our first works over and repent. Someone has to be willing to admit that they had things wrong. If you only meet in the church building to talk about God and you are never doing any outreach, how is that showing the love of God? The story is about more than the son leaving, but the love of his father towards him and the rewards the son received when he came back. In spite of what he did, he was still his father's child.

Romans 5:8 says,
But God commendeth his love toward us, in that, while we were yet sinners, Christ died for us.

I remember going through in my mind asking, "Why does God love me? How can God love a person like me? Why would God let someone like me live?" I remember one of my friends while I was going through my process. I witnessed this man get murdered, and I felt as though God made a mistake because I was the bad guy. I thought It should have been me. I realized at that moment that God was showing me His Love, although I deserved death. My Father loved me too much to allow me to suffer that, so He gave me mercy one more time. If God desired to kill me, He could have let it happen so many times, even though He knew I wasn't going to get my act together right away, He is longsuffering towards us. That's Love!

Many days, I wondered why God put up with my sins, the problems, and the struggles I had. In the story of the prodigal son, when the father saw the son afar off, he was overwhelmed with joy. The son was fearful, he was trying to get his story of repentance together, but unconditional love overtook the situation. God didn't ask all of the details; He already knew them; He forgave him and restored him. My question is, If you repent and God forgives you, why can't you be in operation in the gifts He gave you to use? I'm not talking about someone who is continually going in and out of the church. Someone who has been a co-laborer in the gospel that has returned and is seeking out their salvation with fear and trembling. Is it possible for that person to be restored in the spirit of Love?

Galatians 6:1 says

"Brethren, if a man be overtaken in a fault, ye which are spiritual, restore such an one in the spirit of meekness; considering thyself, lest thou also be tempted."

When God forgives you, He will wrap his arms around you and anoint you. We can't do anything to make Him love us more or less, and His love has no conditions. All our righteousness is as filthy rags, even on our best day, we are still unfit for the kingdom, but because God has unconditional love, nothing you do is going to change the way He feels about you. The song says, "He saw the best in me when everyone else could see the worse in me. He's mine I'm his, he only sees me for what I am." - Marvin Sap

That's unconditional love.

Scriptures To Remember
(The Story of the Prodigal Son)

11 And he said, A certain man had two sons:

12 And the younger of them said to his father, Father, give me the portion of goods that falleth to me. And he divided unto them his living.

13 And not many days after the younger son gathered all together, and took his journey into a far country, and there wasted his substance with riotous living.

14 And when he had spent all, there arose a mighty famine in that land; and he began to be in want.

15 And he went and joined himself to a citizen of that country; and he sent him into his fields to feed swine.

16 And he would fain have filled his belly with the husks that the swine did eat: and no man gave unto him.

17 And when he came to himself, he said, How many hired servants of my father's have bread enough and to spare, and I perish with hunger!

18 I will arise and go to my father, and will say unto him, Father, I have sinned against heaven, and before thee,

19 And am no more worthy to be called thy son: make me as one of thy hired servants.

20 And he arose, and came to his father. But when he was yet a great way off, his father saw him, and had compassion, and ran, and fell on his neck, and kissed him.

21 And the son said unto him, Father, I have sinned against heaven, and in thy sight, and am no more worthy to be called thy son.

22 But the father said to his servants, Bring forth the best robe, and put it on him; and put a ring on his hand, and shoes on his feet:

23 And bring hither the fatted calf, and kill it; and let us eat, and be merry:

24 For this my son was dead, and is alive again; he was lost, and is found. And they began to be merry.

25 Now his elder son was in the field: and as he came and drew nigh to the house, he heard musick and dancing.

26 And he called one of the servants, and asked what these things meant.

27 And he said unto him, Thy brother is come; and thy father hath killed the fatted calf, because he hath received him safe and sound.

28 And he was angry, and would not go in: therefore came his father out, and intreated him.

29 And he answering said to his father, Lo, these many years do I serve thee, neither transgressed I at any time thy commandment: and yet thou never gavest me a kid, that I might make merry with my friends:

30 But as soon as this thy son was come, which hath devoured thy living with harlots, thou hast killed for him the fatted calf.

31 And he said unto him, Son, thou art ever with me, and all that I have is thine.

32 It was meet that we should make merry, and be glad: for this thy brother was dead, and is alive again; and was lost, and is found.

Other Scriptures To Remember

Romans 5:8 says,
But God commendeth his love toward us, in that, while we were yet sinners, Christ died for us.

1 John 4:16 says,
And we have known and believed the love that God hath to us. God is love; and he that dwelleth in love dwelleth in God, and God in him.

St. John 3:16 says,
For God so loved the world, that he gave his only begotten Son, that whosoever believeth in him should not perish, but have everlasting life.

1 John 3:16 says,
Hereby perceive we the love [of God], because he laid down his life for us: and we ought to lay down [our] lives for the brethren.

1 John 4:9-10 says,

In this was manifested the love of God toward us, because that God sent his only begotten Son into the world, that we might live through him. Herein is love, not that we loved God, but that he loved us, and sent his Son [to be] the propitiation for our sins.

New life

We hear so much about having a new life in Christ, but how do we get this new life? A new life starts with having faith in God. I'm not saying you are not a believer, but do you believe you can start over again? Do you believe that God is a rewarder to them that diligently seek Him, even if you messed up? If you come to God, you must first believe that He is! This change does not happen overnight; it's going to take time because we still remember. Looking at my past, it took years for me. I published this book to help someone who is going through what I went through. It might not be on the same scale, but know you can have a new life in Christ. You might say, "I repented, and I am back in church." Know that you can live without condemning yourself for the mistakes of your past. Brush yourself off, get up, and keep moving. You have to pray on yourself that you don't get stuck because of what people think of you, low self-esteem, or because you feel unworthy. Having a new life means sometimes you have to encourage and be a cheerleader to yourself. People can't always look at you and see that something is going on inside of you, but we have a Father who sees everything.

Philippians 3:10&11 says,
"That I may know him, and the power of his resurrection, and the fellowship of his sufferings, being made conformable unto his death; If by any means, I might attain unto the resurrection of the dead."

During this walk with God, we will get knocked down sometimes, but you must get back up. We are running for a prize that we might know Him. People talk about how they got a chance to meet various celebrities, that's nice, but knowing Jesus should be our goal. To know Him, we share in the power of His resurrection and the fellowship of His sufferings. That means we have to go through more than one trial. There are higher heights and deeper depths not only in God but in our appointed pain. We don't go through for no reason; we do all this to know Him. He said, take my yoke upon you and learn of me, for my yoke is easy, and my burdens are light, and you shall have rest for your soul. The devil offers you death, but Jesus comes that we might have life and have it more abundantly.

Philippians 3:13&14 says,

Brethren, I count not myself to have apprehended: but this one thing I do, forgetting those things which are behind, and reaching forth unto those things which are before, I press toward the mark for the prize of the high calling of God in Christ Jesus.

It doesn't feel good when people talk about you and treat you like an outcast. Forget about it! Stop letting those thoughts run across your mind. That's the suffering! What about having to look saints in the face, and you know they are talking about you behind your back, mistreating you. That's letting your flesh die to self. The goal is to obtain the resurrection of life, not the approval of man. Everyone can be against me, as long as God is for me, that's all that matters. These are strong words until you have to go through it yourself. It takes time, but you can make it. I did, don't let anyone dim your light, go through the way God intends, so you come out on another level. Learn something from this experience; let it take you higher. Learn to embrace the Father because He is waiting to welcome you. You aren't some hired servant, you are a son, and you have rights as a son.

Scriptures to Remember

Lamentations 3:22-24 says,
It is of the LORD's mercies that we are not consumed, because his compassions fail not. They are new every morning: great is thy faithfulness.

Isaiah 43:18-19 says,
Remember ye not the former things, neither consider the things of old. Behold, I will do a new thing; now it shall spring forth; shall ye not know.

2 Corinthians 5:17 says,
Therefore if any man be in Christ, he is a new creature: old things are passed away; behold, all things are become new.

Galatians 6:14-16 says,
But God forbid that I should glory, save in the cross of our Lord Jesus Christ, by whom the world is crucified unto me, and I unto the world. For in Christ Jesus neither circumcision availeth any thing, nor uncircumcision, but a new creature. And as many as walk according to this rule, peace be on them, and mercy, and upon the Israel of God.

A call to self evaluation

What if someone were to bring up a past fault and keep throwing it in your face every time something went wrong? That should raise some red flags in your mind. Especially if that person were from the household of faith. It's ungodly to keep holding something over a person's head that God Himself has cast into the sea of forgetfulness. The person who does this is doing more harm than they know. I'm not talking about your neighbor or the member at your church; I'm talking about you. For some, it's easier to forgive a person who harmed us than it is to forgive ourselves. When we are unable to move forward, closure becomes delayed, which can make it hard for some to function in daily tasks. I know you might be thinking, why do I have to forgive myself? You give up your right to hold the wrong you've done against yourself, free yourself to move forward in God without walking on eggshells. Know that you may continue to make mistakes, but if you are willing to keep getting up and trying all over again, you can be an overcomer. One of the things the Father has for you is forgiveness, so forgive yourself.

Ecclesiastes 9:11 says,
I returned, and saw under the sun, that the race is not to the swift, nor the battle to the strong, neither yet bread to the wise, nor yet riches to.

The life we live gets compared to a race; we can't win this race if we sabotage ourselves. The Bible says that we should run that we might obtain. Unforgiveness places obstacles and stumbling blocks in our way. These are in addition to the ones that are already on the course. I encourage you to spend some time falling in love with yourself, faults, and all. It's after learning to love yourself that you can love others. Consider pondering this, do you love yourself enough to seek to strive for perfection, casting down every vain imagination and everything that exalts itself against God? I'm not asking you to make a God out of yourself; realize you are made in His image and because you are His ambassador. Strive to be as close to His image as humanly possible.

The song says, "To be like Jesus, to be like Jesus, Oh how I long to be like Him." Although we say we have faith in God, do we have the confidence to believe that He allows us to start all over again? I know this isn't an overnight process, even when you walk the way that God intends, you have a conscience of what you did. That is when your faith has to activate. You believe that God is all-powerful and all-knowing, didn't he know you were going to be where you are today? If He ordained you before time began, did He intend to drop you like a hot potato once you messed up?

Mark 9:24 says,
"Lord, I believe; help thou mine unbelief."

Is it possible that we limit God's forgiveness to the extent of our own? God is longing for the day when we embrace Him as a forgiver and realize the depth of His great and unconditional Love for us. Romans 5:8 says, "But God commendeth his love toward us, in that, while we were yet sinners, Christ died for us." This scripture does not give us a pass to sin, but it should encourage us to get back up again and get it right. Most people get stuck every time they fall because they view God as some dictator who is waiting for them to fall. It's the contrary He is our Father, and He desires that all come to repentance, even if it takes a little longer for some than others. What you do and who you surround yourself with can make or break you. As Christians, we have to read, pray, be around like-minded individuals, and forgive ourselves beyond what our minds can comprehend. An example from the

Bible is when King David said his sins were always before him.

> Psalms 51:3 says,
> *"For I acknowledge my transgressions: and my sin is ever before me."*

It's good to be mindful of the wrong that you did so you won't repeat it, but when it keeps playing over and over in your mind, that's torment. Renewing your mind daily through fasting, praying, worship, praise, and godly fellowship will help you break these cycles of torture the enemy wishes to keep you stuck in.

These screens are always playing out in our minds. When we pray, fast, go to church and praise God, it gives us more power than we know. The devil is before the throne day and night accusing us, but we know that God can cast our sins in the sea of forgetfulness. I know I said it earlier, but isn't it nice to know that God won't remember something that my brother or sister in Christ might throw in my face later? If you look at me and only see my past faults, then you are outside of the will of God. If we forgive like we want God to forgive us, how can we look at a person and even think in our hearts, "I remember when..." When you see me, you should see through the eyes of God, which is the eyes of Love.

As the Apostle Paul said in Hebrews 13:1 Let brotherly love continue. We say we want to be like Jesus, Jesus would love His brother. If old things are passed away and I have become new, then I'm pardoned. If I see you, I should be able to see Love abiding on the inside so much that I feel it. We need to love the weak, is it too much to ask for the body of Christ that we walk in the newness of life, and restore backsliders in the spirit of meekness.

Let the power of love work. Love is what Love does! Love restores, It died for us, Love came from out of glory and wrapped Itself in a body saying, "Father, if thou be willing, remove this cup from me: nevertheless not my will, but thine, be done." Love sacrificed everything for the lost. It's sad, but some saints are like Pharisees, trying so hard to get the law down to the letter that we forget to Love. We forget the value and importance of one soul that repents.

Its all part of the process we have to go through. Stop worrying about what others are thinking of you. That's why some people don't come to church. Many churches make a huge deal about things that aren't doctrine. As a society, we have become entangled with this worldly idea of how "The Church" should look. Not to mention the drama that we see aired on television, that is not God's church. We have this "Church" thing wrong.

The individuals are the church, not the building. How dare we reverence the building more than the individuals. In the Bible, we have priestly garments but no "Church clothes." What is church clothes for the laymen? It's not in the Bible. We wonder why pews are empty. People aren't coming because (1) I don't have money (2) I don't have church clothes, we have created an environment where others feel intimidated walking in the house of God. How can we stand before God if we are chasing people away with the tradition of men?

After returning to God, I saw people in high positions, and I felt ashamed because I wasn't in the place where I felt like I could be. I had to learn to stay in my lane, in my process. Too often, we base our lives off of someone else's process. I have to go about it differently. This walk is about growing and trusting, not saying that we won't stumble or fall. We have to ask ourselves, are we willing to get back up again? Are we willing to endure until the end?

A challenge to change

As Christians, we live a life where we should always be growing. I faced many challenges when it came to remembering, but I had to push through my shortcomings and feelings of insecurity. God helped me through it, and He can help you too. I keep saying it because it's needed, don't expect this to happen overnight, yeah, you confessed, but you might miss the mark again and again before you get it right. Don't try to rush it, and don't get so frustrated that you give up, press your way through and keep going. They have a saying, "Practice makes perfect." You don't get good at something you only do a few times, in school, you have to continually practice your work until you can do it without thinking.

Holiness is a lifestyle if you have been sinning for 15 years, and you have a habit that is deeply rooted, the enemy has a stronghold on your life, but God is a deliverer! I'm not saying you are going to fall every day; you will have good days and bad days. It all comes back to the process. You may stumble, but get it right. Keep going back to God. You are not like everyone else; our testimonies are different. God may deliver one saint instantly, and you have to work at that same issue, both of you are His children. David said, his foot almost slipped when he beheld the prosperity of the wicked. If you are not careful, when you are coming back to God, your feet can slip, watching the success of the ones who are living for God, while comparing yourself to them.

We are in the middle of a battle, this is a fight, and your day is coming. How do you know that this is not part of your reaping? The truth of the matter is you sold yourself out and now you have to struggle to regain what you had. The first time God gave it to you, now you have to work to get it back. God wants you to know how hard it is to get back so you can appreciate where He has you. When you see how easy it is to fall from grace and how hard it is to get back, you are less likely to make that mistake twice. In the process, learn how to encourage yourself in the Lord. Remember to love and tell your self that you can make it.

Don't get so ashamed that you don't open up about what you are going through. You can't get help until you ask. Stop telling everyone about you; everyone cannot handle you. Most people who love you and walk with you on the mountain won't come close to you in your valley. Now is the time to stop exposing yourself to everyone. Pray to God for someone you can trust and open yourself up to, and remember God desires to take your burdens, you no longer have to carry the hurt. Prayer is the key; when we communicate to God, He will lead us through the fire and the flood.

God lead Israel through the water; He was a cloud by day and fire by night. When you see the clouds, we know that God is present. When you are on your way back, if you see that things are hard, look up. God is in the midst of his church; the church is God's precious jewel. Sometimes you have to drive the devil out, and sometimes we have to cast him out. Stop thinking the worse about things. Sometimes I have to tell myself, "The devil believes God more for me than I do;" that's why he tries to sidetrack me. Have faith in God; He can tell the end from the beginning. He already said we were more than conquerors.

God loves you, and He has a plan for you. Jesus came so we can have an abundant life, one that doesn't include us living with the torments of our past. The problem is sinning is wrong, and it separates us from God, but we have an advocate with the Father, our Father. The result of sin in the present is spiritual separation from God, but after a while, eternal separation from God. My brother and sister, I would not let the thoughts of others make me miss out on what God has for me.

I want to end this book with a challenge to give God more. Maybe it's been hard for you to give God all of you. Make a choice today; choose that this is not where your story ends. Make a decision today to start earnestly awaiting His return.

1 Thessalonians 4:16-17 says,
For the Lord himself shall descend from heaven with a shout, with the voice of the archangel, and with the trump of God: and the dead in Christ shall rise first: Then we which are alive and remain shall be caught up together with them in the clouds, to meet the Lord in the air: and so shall we ever be with the Lord.

God is returning for a church without spot or wrinkle or any such thing. I urge you to make sure you are in a right relationship with God, don't let it be said too late in your case. The people who shun you away; they won't be standing before God with you; every person will have to see God for themselves. God's arms are open wide; He is not willing that any should perish, but that all come to repentance. Remember, repentance is a daily thing; it can happen right now.

Acts 2:38 says,

Then Peter said unto them, Repent, and be baptized every one of you in the name of Jesus Christ for the remission of sins, and ye shall receive the gift of the Holy Ghost.

Notes

Notes

Notes

Notes

Sponsor

I would like to thank my sponsor who helped absorb some of the cost of getting this project completed. Please show your support to

Apostle Charles E Waters 3rd, LLC

(advertisement on next page)

Charles E. Waters 3rd, LLC

An International Prophetic Ministry which lives by its standard of Sudden Victory.

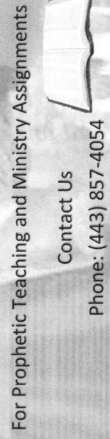

For Prophetic Teaching and Ministry Assignments

Contact Us

Phone: (443) 857-4054

Email: sahgee3@gmail.com

Facebook: Charles E Waters, III

"The Kingdom of God raises our Standard of Belief."

Read with a friend

Most people read alone, but as you can see from the contents of this book, it is not just something to pass the time. The words in this book can minister life to the reader. I ask that you consider reading this with a friend.

Do you know a backslider? Consider purchasing a copy for them. It can help them to work out their soul salvation with fear and trembling. This book is not only just a testimony but a plea. Thank you for helping me to spread the good news of what God has done for me and what He wants to do in the lives of so many others.

Jeffrey Briscoe

Made in the USA
Middletown, DE
02 October 2024